The Preppers Apocalypse Survival Guide to Everyday Carry or EDC and PSK

I0422006

Steve Rayder

Steve Rayder

SOUTHSHORE
PUBLICATIONS & DISTRIBUTION

www.southshorepublications.com

ISBN- 978-1512144321

ISBN-10: 1512144320

CONTENTS

1. WHAT IS AN EDC AND A PSK?

EDC stands for Every Day Carry. It is essentially a set of personalized items that you carry on you every day.

This can be gear that you carry in case of some kind of emergency, or just a set of items that you carry to make your day to day life easier. Of course some things fit into both categories, and your EDC can be tailored to suit both of these scenarios.

PSK stands for Pocket Survival Kit and is a less commonly used term in the Survival and Preparedness community.

Almost everyone in the world has an EDC whether they know it or not. A wallet, a phone and keys are all Every Day Carry items. In the Prepping world however, we take things a step further to both customize these items to add to their functionality and also by adding new items to this list.

Organizing and tailoring your EDC to suit your individual needs will ideally make your everyday tasks more efficient and also stand you in good stead if some kind of emergency situation were to occur.

There are many different types of EDC and no two people will have the exact same kit, because you will pick and choose the items you think best and the most worthwhile to suit your particular needs.

Over the course of this book I will go into the various aspects that you should consider when planning your EDC and PSK, also providing some great tips on some extremely compact, multiuse items that you may not have considered that are perfect for EDC's.

Steve Rayder

2. MICRO EDC KITS

A micro EDC kit is pretty much what it says on the tin, a very small EDC that can easily fit in your pocket. Micro EDC's are usually contained within a tin or small pouch of some kind to keep everything compact and organized.

Now there's no real substitute for having a good sized knife or a decent multi-tool when you need one. However, carrying a heavy metal multi-tool and a knife every day can be a bit of a pain. You can attach things in pouches on your belt but I find that's also a bit of an inconvenience.

Of course you may not mind carrying full sized items. Or you may regularly carry some sort of bag that you can put these items into. But if you did want to cut things down to size a bit and go more compact, let's go over some of the options.

Firstly, for a micro EDC, you are going to want some kind of tin or pouch. A lot of Preppers will use an Altoids tin. These tiny mint tins measure about 2.35 x 3.75 inches making them small enough to fit comfortably into anybody's pocket. The dilemma is how to fit everything into it. Luckily there are ways around this.

As far as pouches go, there are a whole variety of mini pouches you can use to store everything. But if you want some recommendations to use as a starting point then the Micro Pocket Organizer by Maxpedition will work well for most people, although they are larger than an Altoids tin at 5.5 inches long.

I also once saw someone using an earbuds case that was actually slightly smaller than an Altoids tin. The zipper that ran around 3 sides of the pouch and the inner mesh pockets made the earbud pouch a perfect micro EDC case. The best thing to do is just have a shop about on Amazon and you should be able to find something perfect for you.

If you're unsure of whether you should go for a tin or a pouch there are a couple of advantages for each. Tins will offer a slightly more water resistant container and will also offer more protection for the contents than the fabric of a pouch. Also tins such as Altoids tins have bare metal surfaces both inside and out which can be polished and used as a mirror. Mirrors are extremely useful for signaling and first aid applications. However pouches have a bit of give and will stretch slightly making them easier to fit the items into. They will also generally feel better in your pocket than a metal tin and the items inside are far less likely to rattle in your pocket.

Talking of rattling, a little tip if you are having a problem with this is to get a pack of tiny rare earth magnets and some glue. You can attach the magnets to the items that are ratting about and attach them to the inside of the tin, ensuring everything stays in place.

What you actually keep in your Micro EDC kit is completely up you, but I have a few tips on how to keep the weight and size of the items in your micro kit as low as possible.

With these micro kits it's more about compromising on functionality to save space and weight more than anything else. As well as of course efficiently packing your kit in way that makes the best use of the space you have available. Therefore, many of the items that fit into such a small kit may not be what you would ideally want to be carrying with you, but they will still do the job that you need them to.

So to start with a lot of people like to keep a pen and a notepad in their EDC. In a micro kit you could just keep one or two notepad pages folded up instead of a full notepad, chances are you're not going to need more than that throughout the course of the day anyway. As for the pen, you could consider either a telescopic pen or for a cheaper and even lighter option, you could get a small ball point refill and just use that to write with.

If you want to keep a knife, you're going to have to choose a very small one. This is one area where I wouldn't skimp on quality though. A good quality folding knife with a one inch blade for example shouldn't set you back too much and you be a perfect fit for one of these kits. If you prefer not to keep a knife then you can get a good pair of small, fold up scissors that will fit nicely into this type of kit.

For medical and first aid purposes obviously plasters won't take up much space and are a good idea. For larger wounds you can easily fit in a larger individually packed adhesive bandage. Alcohol swabs are also very compact and easily kept in a small case.

Pry bars are also a popular item for many preppers. You can find very small pry bars that will easily fit into a micro EDC but why stop at a basic pry bar? Some of these types of tool such as the Gerber Artifact also have a few screwdrivers, a bottle opener and a small knife all combined into the pry bar design.

A much overlooked, and very small, item that I think everyone should include in this type of kit is the humble safety pin. They have a million and one uses and I carry at least one safety pin with me at all times.

If you want to keep a multitool then you could do far worse than the Leatherman Squirt. At 1.9oz ad 2.25 inches long it packs a lot of functionality into a small package and as it's made by Leatherman, you know you can trust the quality. Other options include the Leatherman Micra or the knifeless Leatherman Style if you didn't want to carry any kind of blade on you.

Tape is always handy to have and duct tape is the choice of most Preppers due to its strength and water resistant properties. Now obviously can't fit a whole role of duct tape in one of these kits, but you could take a length and fold it into a flat strip. That way you will have a flat, compact strip of heavy duty tape.

You may want to keep some form of lighting in your kit, although most people prefer to keep on on their keychain. If you did want a backup for your micro EDC, I will discuss your options for a good quality small flashlight later in the book.

Finally, fire lighting. Everybody knows you can get small lighters but what some people may not have heard of is a Fresnel lens. These are essentially credit card shaped magnifying lenses. Ideal for a backup form of fire lighting.

3. AN EDC IN A WALLET

Depending on your personal EDC requirements, you may not even need to keep anything on you that doesn't easily fit in your wallet.

There are all kinds of different multi use tools and generally useful items that are made to credit card size, specifically to fit into a wallet.

Also, some of the other items you may want to carry are fairly flat anyway and so are well suited to just put straight into your wallet. Thing such as bandages, alcohol swabs, safety pins, note paper, etc.

As for a multitool, there are simple, flat metal tools you can buy made from a solid piece of steel, with a variety of different functions depending on the tool you choose. This unbranded tool has all of the basic tools such as a bottle opener, screw drivers, a blade, a saw, can opener, etc.

There is also another type of multitool in the shape of a credit card. These are usually made from some kind of plastic and the tools slot in and out of them.

Recommendations for specific tools of this variety to look at, if this sounds like something you would be interested in, would be the Victorinox SwissCard and the SOG Credit Card Companion.

The SwissCard includes a letter opener blade, scissors, a nail file, a screwdriver, tweezers, a toothpick, a pressurized ballpoint pen and a ruler. SOG is more of a well-known name in the Prepping world and provide high quality items. Their Credit Card Companion offers a bottle opener, a can opener, a 2-inch serrated blade, a 8x power magnifying glass, a compass, a ruler, a toothpick and some tweezers. So you get a lot of functionality in both of these items, perfect for an EDC kit.

As I mentioned in the last chapter Fresnel lenses are flat and credit card sized. This means that they are an ideal fire making solution for a wallet kit, although I wouldn't reply on this for your only form of fire lighting because obviously you do need a decent amount of sunlight to use them.

You're going to be pretty when it comes to lighting options but you could opt for an LED Flashlight Card. They aren't the brightest thing around. But they will provide you with light if you are in a pinch.

Steve Rayder

4. EDC KEYCHAINS

This is one of my personal favorite types of EDC. By adding a few simple items to your existing keychain you can add some great functionality easily.

There is a whole host of keychain gadgets that you can choose from these days. The hard part is picking what ones you want and of course knowing when to stop! If you wanted to you could make your keychain your entire EDC. The only thing you can't really add to a keychain easily is medical supplies, although there is a way you could include them.

So in no particular order, I'm going to go through the various items that I would suggest as parts of and EDC keychain.

For the basis of my personal keychain I went for the True Utility TU45 Key Organizer system. It's basically a split ring with 4 really handy quick release clips. It's also has a key section that holds about 4 keys but it's very annoying to use so I removed that part. I have found that in general True Utility isn't the best quality, but the quick release clips on the TU45 are good quality and very useful. For the price, their products are usually pretty good value. So I would definitely recommend it as a good starting point to add all of your other items onto.

If you are thinking of making a fairly substantial sized keychain then you could opt for a wire keychain cable. This will give you a nice large, flexible loop that will fit far more than a traditional split ring.

USB flash drives come in really handy for transferring files and data on the go. You can get some really tiny flash drives these days too, and when I say tiny I mean it. The smaller the better when it comes to keychain EDC's in my opinion because of the obvious SAWC or Size and Weight Constraints. The Kingston DataTraveler is of metal construction and is a very popular choice.

As far as a keychain multitool goes. I find they are a bit too cumbersome and heavy for every day purposes, even a Swiss Army Knife as opposed to a plier design are a bit too clunky for me. The best type of multi tool to go for in this scenario in my opinion is the solid metal pry bar style tools such as the Gerber Artifact which I mentioned earlier in the book.

If you want to keep a method of fire lighting on your keychain then there is a whole range of keychain lighters that work great. Obviously you could just keep a lighter in your pocket but, let's face it, somehow they always seem to go missing after people "borrow" them. If it's on your keychain then it's not going anywhere and you will always have a method of making fire should you need it.

Probably the most popular lighter keychain is the Firestash by True Utility. The Firestash is basically a small cylindrical Zippo style lighter. The great thing about these lighters, and the advantage they have over a standard Zippo, is that they have a rubber o-ring around the cap and the body of the lighter making them waterproof. This also means that the lighter fluid doesn't evaporate over time as easily which is a huge problem with Zippos. Also something that most people don't realize is that these lighters will run on a whole host of fuels, from gasoline to methylated spirits

You can also get ferro rod keychains or just put a ferro rod on your keychain as it is. If you have a lighter however I think there's no need for a ferro rod as an EDC item. If you did want one then a fantastic, compact ferro road/striker combination product is the Bear Grylls Compact Fire Starter.

A good way that you can include a few medical supplies on your keychain is by using one of the cash holder keychains available on the market, that are designed for holding rolled up money such as the True Utility Cashstash. They could also easily be used to contain some rolled up bandages with some tape or something similar. Or they could be used to store a few aspirin or other types of pill. So having a couple of these with some basic medical supplies is the best way I have found to incorporate medical supplies into a keychain.

Another good item, and an old classic, that seems to be overlooked by some people is a whistle. These are obviously great for signaling purposes. If you're lost or injured in the woods, or anywhere else for that matter, and need to get someone's attention from a distance then you will probably be wishing you had included one. There are a lot of very small whistles out there, designed for keychain use, that still pack quite a punch for their size.

Lighting is a nice easy one. There are so many keychain lights out there. They are not however all created equal, some are smaller at the expense of brightness, some are more bulky but easier to operate and some are better quality very expensive. So it's really hard to recommend any one flashlight as it depends on what you personally want. A couple of things I would suggest looking for though are: easy one handed operation, obviously LED rather than a traditional bulb, a strobe function and a carbineer or clip attachment (could always add one yourself).

I will go over product recommendations and talk about flashlights in a bit more detail in the flashlight chapter later in the book.

If you're going for a survival style keychain you can include a military can opener such as the P-38. These can openers are very small and lightweight making them perfect for a keychain, and the military have been using them since 1980 so they must be doing something right.

Also along the survival lines, you may want to consider a small compass keychain. These smaller compasses aren't known to be the most accurate things in the world but they are better than wondering blindly through the woods and going round in circles.

Tweezers are a very useful item to have for a lot of things. The best tweezers I have found, especially for a keychain, are the Uncle Bill's Silver Grippers. They go to a sharp point making them great for precision tasks and splinter removal. They have a handy locking cap to clip the tweezers into on your keychain and stop the sharp points from stabbing you in the leg.

There's a large range of keychain knives out there. I personally don't carry a dedicated knife, but what I do carry is a Utilikey. A Utilikey is a key shaped piece of metal that blends in with the rest of your keys and is pretty unnoticeable to anyone that isn't looking for it. When you need to use the Utilikey you simply pull the two halves of the key apart and it comes off of the keychain revealing a small a knife/saw blade, along with a bottle opener and a couple of screwdrivers. It's a great little item and although it's not the sharpest thing in the world, I have found it to come in very handy indeed.

Another item you may want to consider is a P7 suspension clip. This basically allows you to clip your keys onto your pocket meaning that, if your keychain is getting a bit bulky, it won't all just bunch up in the bottom of your pocket giving you a big, annoying keychain bulge.

5. EDC AND PSK ON A BUDGET

If you're on a budget and you want to put together a cheap and cheerful kit, just so you have something to get you started, then this chapter is for you.

You can always add to your kit and upgrade items as you go. For now you don't need to go all out and spend hundreds on a top of the range multitool and a gleaming new knife. The basics will go just fine for now.

So there are four main four areas most people want to cover in their EDC's and PSK's are: a knife/multitool, first aid, a light source and a method of lighting a fire. These things are all pretty easy to cover on even the tightest of budgets.

A great starting point for your budget EDC kit is those mini first aid kits. Because not only do you get some first aid supplies, you also get the pouch which you can use to store all of your other EDC items in if you want to. They are also incredibly cheap from most places.

So that will cover most of your basic first aid needs, as these things usually contain bandages and gauzes etc. I would recommend adding some alcohol wipes if there isn't any included and that will about cover it, unless you want to throw any aspirin in there for example. So all of that should be very cheap indeed.

There are a whole host of different types of budget multitool on the market. The one thing I would strongly suggest is to get a plier type multitool rather than the Swiss army style, purely for the fact that they have far more functionality and the pliers are so handy. Unless you get a bladeless multitool, this will also cover your knife situation. If you did want to get a standalone knife then that's entirely up to you.

Fire lighting is an easy one, you can just get a couple of cheap disposable lighters. I say a couple because it's always best to have a backup way of making fire in case your primary method fails. For a far more in depth look into lighters and fire making in general you can take a look at my book on camp fires and fire pits. Shameless self-promotion...check.

An affordable light source is easily sourced. A decent enough quality LED flashlight isn't going to be expensive but they really are worth having on you. Even if you do have a light on your phone, as most people so these days, it's always good to have a flash light as a backup, particularly if this is a Pocket Survival Kit as opposed to an EDC. In a survival situation, not only do you want to save your battery for contacting people, but you also want to have a long lasting backup in case your phone battery dies.

Another cheap addition you could add to your budget kit is some jute twine. Very cheap and easy to fit into a kit. Not only can it be used as cordage for throwing up a shelter or making repairs, it can also be fluffed up and used as a makeshift tinder. This is particularly useful for fire lighting in poor weather conditions when all of the natural tinder is wet.

Personally I would also consider adding a space blanket as they are so cheap and they can save your life if you're stuck out in the cold. They can also be used in conjunction with the jute twine to rig up some form of shelter over your head if you need to.

That's really all you need to get you started, just a few cheap items that almost anyone can afford. As I said, you can upgrade it as and when you feel like it, but this is a great starting point.

6. SELF DEFENSE ITEMS

When most people think if self-defense items they will instantly think of something like a gun or a combat knife. I personally would not expect to run into a situation where I would get into a life or death knife fight or shoot out on a daily basis, therefore I would not include either in my EDC.

For those of you who do want to carry a gun, I'm sure you know that you would only use it as a last ditch option if you were in a life or death scenario anyway. I just don't see a gun as being needed in an EDC personally, but if you do, then that's completely up to you.

There are however a lot of other items that would give you a huge advantage in a combat situation that I am going to talk about in this chapter.

What you are able to carry depends on exactly what country or state you live in so remember to check the laws for the area you are in before carrying any kind of weapon with you. Some people may be legally entitled to keep a gun with them, where as in some other places, carrying a knife with a blade longer than an inch may be illegal.

The same laws apply on sprays and Tasers, in a lot of places pepper spray is legal, in the UK however both of these things are illegal and reserved for use by the police force.

A good self-defense option is to get yourself a monkey fist keychain. If you have never heard of a money fist before, it's essentially a paracord keychain but with a fairly large ball bearing hidden under a ball of paracord in the end. These things are a very effective weapon. To use them, all you have to do is hold your keys in your hand and leave the monkey fist hanging free and swing it at your attacker. This extends your reach and the pendula motion of the swinging ball bearing increases the impact velocity too. Obviously these give you some emergency cordage too if you need it and they are a really good glass breaker.

I would definitely recommend pepper spray or something similar for a few reasons. Firstly and most importantly, it will pretty much fully incapacitate an attacker quickly and easily allowing you to escape a dangers situation. But probably the main advantage of pepper spray for me is that it's non-lethal. I'm sure we can all agree that if we had the choice out of stopping an attacker in their tracks and getting away unharmed is a much better option than shooting or stabbing them and potentially being sent to jail for defending yourself.

Pepper spray does have the obvious and much discussed disadvantage of potentially being blown back in your own face. It's well known for affecting anyone nearby as well as the person it is being used on. Also, sometimes pepper spray just won't stop your attacker. Granted this is only usually when they are on some pretty crazy drugs, but it does happen. So it's not perfect, but I still think it's a good option. Especially because with most people, all you would have to do it point it at them and they would back off.

You can get pepper spray in all kinds of strengths and sizes so have a shop about and see what suits you best. Even some of the really small pocket sizes sprays have over 20 hits in them, so you can easily get away with something small and discrete that you can carry on you every day.

As I mentioned, in some places such as the UK and in some states, pepper spray is illegal. However there are some sprays that are known as criminal identifiers that are completely legal as they contain no irritants. Now that may seem like the whole point of pepper spray, the fact that the irritants get into your eyes and airways, but having a foam sprayed into your face when you are trying to attack someone is still going to be very distracting and can also temporarily impair vision. This should give you enough time to get away or, if you can't get away, to bring out your monkey fist keychain and use it.

The other great thing about criminal identifier sprays such as Farb Spray are that they stain whatever they touch, including skin, bright red for weeks. This stuff doesn't wash off. This is where they get their name, because it makes the police's job in successfully identifying your attacker so much easier. Now you are probably thinking, well they could just lay low for a few weeks until the dye fades. But the thing they probably don't realize is that once the dye has gone, their skin will still glow under an ultraviolet light for another few weeks after that.

Telescopic and spring batons are also a handy piece of kit to have. If you know how to use one properly then they can become very effective indeed. If you are going to carry a baton then I would highly recommend training with it, there are training videos out there that you can follow along with to know how to use them safety. Although just having something to extend your reach and use as a blunt force weapon will give you an advantage. A good baton will have no problem breaking an arm for example so they are not to be underestimated or used lightly.

Another couple of options are SAP gloves and brass knuckles, the obvious drawback being that you need to either have them on or quickly put them on. So they will need to be easily accessed and I personally wouldn't want to have either in my pockets as they are too heavy and cumbersome. But I think they are still worth mentioning as they may be a good solution for some people. I'm sure we all know about brass knuckles but the gloves aren't so common. Basically SAP gloves have some sort knuckle impact protection usually combined with steel or lead shot to add weight. If you get punched by someone with a SAP glove on, you're most probably hitting the deck in one punch.

Lastly, we have the Taser. Obviously there are legal issues and some people may not be able to legally carry them, but Tasers are actually more widely legal than pepper spray. They have come down a lot in price over recent years too, making them easily available to most people.

There are two main types of Taser, a close range stun gun and long range Taser. With the short range stun guns, you can use them repeatedly and they hurt, but they aren't going to stop someone who is really determined. Also you have to get into a close combat situation to be able to use them. With the long range Tasers that fire 2 barbed pins, they have the advantage of being effective at a range of up to 25ft in some cases and they will more often than not, put even the biggest people on the ground. However, each cartridge is only single shot, so you have one chance to hit your target unless you have time to load another cartridge.

Out of the two I would personally go for the long range Taser as they are so much more effective. If you want to see just how effective they are, take a look at some of the reaction videos on YouTube. The other great thing about Tasers is that once you have hit your target, you can drop the Taser and escape while the target is still one the ground being shocked by the Taser for the next 30 seconds.

Also, if you have a Taser, that's probably going to be enough of a deterrent to any would be attacker. So just as with pepper spray, you may not even have to use it. Just point it at them and shout "Taser!" and I don't know about you, but I would be getting out of there as fast as possible if I had one pointed at me.

All this talk of Tasers actually leads me on to the next chapter about flashlights very nicely believe it or not.

7. FLASHLIGHTS

For EDC purposes you don't want to be carrying a lot so multi-use items are a big advantage. So something that multi-use and is a legal carry weapon pretty much anywhere is the world, is a flashlight. You may be wondering how a flash light can be an effective weapon. Well there are some pretty heavy, solidly constructed, tactical flash lights out there that are perfectly designed for combat with a strike bezel around the top or bottom of the light. These can be used very effectively as a blunt force weapon.

We can however go one step further. There are now Taser flashlights on the market such as the VIPERTEK VTS-195, that add yet another level of functionality by basically turning your flashlight into a stun gun at the flick of a switch (not quite so legal in a lot of places). The noise of these things is pretty scary alone. If someone is attacking you and you pull out a flashlight that suddenly started flashing and making loud, crackling electrical noises then you're going to look like James Bond and that's going to be a fairly potent deterrent.

Torches can also help you in another way in a combat situation. If you get an especially bright torch with a strobe function, in low light conditions you can actually strobe any potential assailant offering you a big advantage. You would be surprised at how much of a difference a strobe can make if you have never had someone come at you with one before. I actually have had this happen to me during a game of airsoft in a dark bunker and, if you're not expecting it, the strobe renders you pretty useless for at least a good few seconds.

Self-defense and combat uses aside, flashlights are obviously very useful for general lighting purposes and are a good item to have. If you didn't want to go for a large tactical flashlight as described above then that's up to personal preference because they aren't for everyone. A lot of people just want something compact that offers a bit of light when they need it. In which case you can opt for something much smaller that will easily fit into your kit.

Steve Rayder

8. CORDAGE

For EDC purposes, if you do want to carry cordage, you probably wouldn't want to be lugging about a lot of paracord. Fortunately there are a few other options.

The first is to simply store your paracord in a space saving way. I'm sure most of you have seen the paracord bracelets that are available or that you can make yourself. This is a good way of keeping some good cordage on you at all times, but it's not for me as I don't like wearing them. As I mentioned previously in the keychain chapter, you can also buy or make paracord keychain fobs, there are much more my cup of tea and don't take up a lot of extra space. So that's one way of doing it.

You could also take the drastic plunge and not use paracord, shock horror! Yes that's right, the good old Prepper favorite of paracord may not be the best option for EDC purposes.

Obviously if we are going to be carrying something round with us, we want them to be light and compact. Paracord isn't exactly the most light and compact thing going. Kevlar chord however, is about a third of the thickness, meaning it takes up less space and is also therefore lighter than paracord. Bearing in mind its thinner, it can actually provide far greater strength than paracord too.

Your average 550 paracord is about 6mm thick and has a breaking strain of, you guessed it, 550lbs. A piece of Kevlar chord that is 2mm thick can have a breaking strain of 950lb. Considering

Paracord is known for its weight to strength ratio, I would say that's pretty impressive numbers on the Kevlar cords part.

Also paracord does have some stretch to it which can be a disadvantage in some situations and the Kevlar is also far more heat resistant. Having said this, paracord is a lot cheaper than Kevlar and it's much easier to work with as it has a nicer texture with more grip to it when compared to the slightly more slippery feeling Kevlar. So I would personally still go for Paracord in most situations, but if you want some light and compact cordage for an EDC or PSK that is incredibly strong then Kevlar cord is a great option.

A space saving, multi-use item that you could also consider is Fire Cord. This type of cordage that, while maintaining a similar strength to width ratio of paracord, also has a waterproof, flammable inner strand. You can easily cut off a section of this cord and remove the flammable red strand. This cord can be lit as it is, or you can fluff it out a bit and it will easily take a spark from a ferro rod.

9. MEDICAL SUPPLIES

EDC and PSK style medical kits are usually small and lightweight due to size and weight constraints. There are a lot of pre-made medical kits out there, and they're good to have, but they can be a bit on the bulky side. So I would say it's best to make your own based on how much you personally want to carry with you.

The first thing you need to decide is what type of medical kit are you going to be putting together? You could just go for something basic, mainly concerned with minor bleeding, cuts and lacerations. Or you could go for something more advanced that deals with more major wounds and hypothermia too.

So let's start with the first kind of kit I mentioned that is just really concerned with minor lacerations. For a very basic kit, all you're going to need is a few alcohol swabs, some band-aids, some sterile gauzes and some tape. You may as well go for some antibiotic band-aids as they can really help with preventing infections in the generally unsanitary conditions of a survival situation. But I would say that's pretty much all you need for day to day usage. This will take up hardly any room at all so it's very practical.

I would also always recommend keeping a pair of disposable gloves in case you have to treat someone else. I personally don't want to be getting a strangers blood on me if I had to help them out. A pair of disposable gloves takes up such little space and weigh hardly anything that they are definitely worth having in my opinion.

If you want to cover the treatment of deeper wounds then there is a couple more items you could add. If a deep wound is sustained to an arm or a leg, one of the best items to have is a tourniquet. This may be a bit much for everyday use, as realistically it's very rare that you would come across a wound that bad in your day to day life. But if you did want to carry one with you then the SWAT-T Tourniquet is very compact and will slip into most med kits easily.

Another option, or something that you could combine with the tourniquet for a much more effective solution, is a Quikclot product like the Quikclot Sport 50 Gram. You basically use this like a medical gauze and apply it directly to the wound and secure it in place. This really is an amazing product, it uses the naturally occurring enzyme that promotes blood clotting. You can easily use one of these on yourself, meaning you can easily treat major bleeding without any help. Just make sure you have some type of compression bandage in your kit too so that you can secure it in place.

I would usually include a couple of space/foil blankets in my kit somewhere. Obviously there are great for keeping yourself, or someone you are treating warm and can come in really handy so I would definitely advise you to carry one in your medical kit if you have room.

Steve Rayder

10. FINAL THOUGHTS

Well I think that about overs it for this installment of the Preppers Apocalypse Survival Guide!

If you want to stay up to date with my regular free book promotions and to also find out about my future releases you can sign up to my mailing list at - www.southshorepublications.com/steverayder

If you would also consider taking the time to leave me an honest review on this book on Amazon I would be extremely appreciative of your feedback.

You can find links to all of my previous books at - http://www.amazon.com/Steve-Rayder/e/B00U0U3Z3E/ or by searching for "Steve Rayder" on Amazon.

Thanks for reading and I hopefully speak to you all in the next book!

Steve Rayder

www.ingramcontent.com/pod-product-compliance
Lightning Source LLC
Chambersburg PA
CBHW070844290526
45795CB00002B/976